SCUBA
Diving
Log Book

THIS BOOK BELONGS TO :

NAME : ....

PHONE : ....

ADDRESS : ....

DATE :	
DIVE # :	
COUNTRY :	
LOCATION :	
VISIBILITY :	
WEIGHT :	
CURRENT :	

CONDITIONS :

☀️ ☐   ☁️ ☐   🌧️ ☐   ⛅ ☐

🌡️ HOT ☐   🌡️ MIDL ☐   🌡️ CLOUD ☐

😃 ☐   🙂 ☐   ☹️ ☐

○ SALT   ○ FRESH   ○ SHORE   ○ BOAT   ○ DEEP   ○ NIGHT

DIVE DATA :

TIME IN : ....   TIME OUT : ....

MAX DEPTH : ....

BAR/PS : ....   BAR/PS : ....

TIME OUT : ....   TOTAL TIME : ....

VERIFICATION

VERIFICATION SIGNATURE :

☐ INSTRUCTOR   ☐ DIVEMASTER   ☐ BUDDY

NOTES

....
....
....
....
....
....
....

DATE :	**CONDITIONS :**
DIVE # :	☀ ☁ 🌧 ⛅
COUNTRY :	□ □ □ □
LOCATION :	HOT MIDL CLOUD
VISIBILITY :	□ □ □
WEIGHT :	😃 🙂 ☹
CURRENT :	□ □ □

◯ SALT ◯ FRESH ◯ SHORE ◯ BOAT ◯ DEEP ◯ NIGHT

DIVE DATA :

TIME IN : ....   TIME OUT : ....

MAX DEPTH : ....

BAR/PS : ....   BAR/PS : ....

TIME OUT : ....   TOTAL TIME : ....

VERIFICATION	NOTES
VERIFICATION SIGNATURE :	....
	....
	....
	....
	....
	....
	....
◯ INSTRUCTOR ◯ DIVEMASTER ◯ BUDDY	

DATE :	
DIVE # :	
COUNTRY :	
LOCATION :	
VISIBILITY :	
WEIGHT :	
CURRENT :	

CONDITIONS :

☀ ☁ 🌧 ⛅
☐ ☐ ☐ ☐

HOT MIDL CLOUD
☐   ☐   ☐

😃   🙂   ☹
☐   ☐   ☐

☐ SALT ☐ FRESH ☐ SHORE ☐ BOAT ☐ DEEP ☐ NIGHT

DIVE DATA :

TIME IN : ....   TIME OUT : ....

MAX DEPTH : ....

BAR/PS : ....   BAR/PS : ....

TIME OUT : ....   TOTAL TIME : ....

VERIFICATION

VERIFICATION SIGNATURE :

NOTES

....
....
....
....
....
....
....
....

☐ INSTRUCTOR   ☐ DIVEMASTER   ☐ BUDDY

DATE :	
DIVE # :	
COUNTRY :	
LOCATION :	
VISIBILITY :	
WEIGHT :	
CURRENT :	

CONDITIONS :

☀ ☁ 🌧 ⛅
☐ ☐ ☐ ☐

HOT   MIDL   CLOUD
☐   ☐   ☐

😃   🙂   ☹
☐   ☐   ☐

○ SALT   ○ FRESH   ○ SHORE   ○ BOAT   ○ DEEP   ○ NIGHT

DIVE DATA :

TIME IN : ....   TIME OUT : ....

MAX DEPTH : ....

BAR/PS : ....   BAR/PS : ....

TIME OUT : ....   TOTAL TIME : ....

VERIFICATION

VERIFICATION SIGNATURE :

NOTES

....
....
....
....
....
....
....
....

☐ INSTRUCTOR   ☐ DIVEMASTER   ☐ BUDDY

DATE :	**CONDITIONS :**
DIVE # :	☀ ☁ 🌧 ⛅
COUNTRY :	☐ ☐ ☐ ☐
LOCATION :	HOT MIDL CLOUD
VISIBILITY :	☐ ☐ ☐
WEIGHT :	😃 🙂 ☹
CURRENT :	☐ ☐ ☐

☐ SALT   ☐ FRESH   ☐ SHORE   ☐ BOAT   ☐ DEEP   ☐ NIGHT

DIVE DATA :

TIME IN : ....   TIME OUT : ....

MAX DEPTH : ....

BAR/PS : ....   BAR/PS : ....

TIME OUT : ....   TOTAL TIME : ....

VERIFICATION	NOTES
VERIFICATION SIGNATURE :	....
	....
	....
	....
	....
	....
	....
	....
☐ INSTRUCTOR ☐ DIVEMASTER ☐ BUDDY	

DATE :	
DIVE # :	
COUNTRY :	
LOCATION :	
VISIBILITY :	
WEIGHT :	
CURRENT :	

CONDITIONS :

☀ ☁ 🌧 ⛅
☐ ☐ ☐ ☐

HOT MIDL CLOUD
☐   ☐   ☐

😃   🙂   ☹
☐   ☐   ☐

○ SALT ○ FRESH ○ SHORE ○ BOAT ○ DEEP ○ NIGHT

DIVE DATA :

TIME IN : .... TIME OUT : ....

MAX DEPTH : ....

BAR/PS : .... BAR/PS : ....

TIME OUT : .... TOTAL TIME : ....

VERIFICATION

VERIFICATION SIGNATURE :

○ INSTRUCTOR ○ DIVEMASTER ○ BUDDY

NOTES

....
....
....
....
....
....
....
....

DATE :
DIVE # :
COUNTRY :
LOCATION :
VISIBILITY :
WEIGHT :
CURRENT :

CONDITIONS :

- ☀ ☐
- ☁ ☐
- 🌧 ☐
- ⛅ ☐

- HOT ☐
- MIDL ☐
- CLOUD ☐

- 😃 ☐
- 🙂 ☐
- ☹ ☐

○ SALT ○ FRESH ○ SHORE ○ BOAT ○ DEEP ○ NIGHT

DIVE DATA :

TIME IN : ....   TIME OUT : ....

MAX DEPTH : ....

BAR/PS : ....   BAR/PS : ....

TIME OUT : ....   TOTAL TIME : ....

VERIFICATION

VERIFICATION SIGNATURE :

☐ INSTRUCTOR   ☐ DIVEMASTER   ☐ BUDDY

NOTES

....
....
....
....
....
....
....
....

DATE :	
DIVE # :	
COUNTRY :	
LOCATION :	
VISIBILITY :	
WEIGHT :	
CURRENT :	

CONDITIONS :

☀ ☁ 🌧 ⛅
☐ ☐ ☐ ☐

HOT   MIDL   CLOUD
☐   ☐   ☐

😀 🙂 ☹
☐ ☐ ☐

○ SALT ○ FRESH ○ SHORE ○ BOAT ○ DEEP ○ NIGHT

DIVE DATA :

TIME IN : ....   TIME OUT : ....

MAX DEPTH : ....

BAR/PS : ....   BAR/PS : ....

TIME OUT : ....   TOTAL TIME : ....

VERIFICATION

VERIFICATION SIGNATURE :

☐ INSTRUCTOR   ☐ DIVEMASTER   ☐ BUDDY

NOTES

....
....
....
....
....
....
....
....

DATE :	**CONDITIONS :**
DIVE # :	☀️ ☁️ 🌧️ ⛅
COUNTRY :	☐ ☐ ☐ ☐
LOCATION :	HOT MIDL CLOUD
VISIBILITY :	☐ ☐ ☐
WEIGHT :	😃 🙂 ☹️
CURRENT :	☐ ☐ ☐

◯ SALT ◯ FRESH ◯ SHORE ◯ BOAT ◯ DEEP ◯ NIGHT

DIVE DATA :

TIME IN : ....   TIME OUT : ....

MAX DEPTH : ....

BAR/PS : ....   BAR/PS : ....

TIME OUT : ....   TOTAL TIME : ....

VERIFICATION	NOTES
VERIFICATION SIGNATURE :	....
	....
	....
	....
	....
	....
	....
	....
☐ INSTRUCTOR ☐ DIVEMASTER ☐ BUDDY	

DATE :	**CONDITIONS :**
DIVE #	☀ ☁ 🌧 ⛅
COUNTRY :	□ □ □ □
LOCATION :	HOT MIDL CLOUD
VISIBILITY :	□ □ □
WEIGHT :	☺ ☺ ☹
CURRENT :	□ □ □

◯ SALT   ◯ FRESH   ◯ SHORE   ◯ BOAT   ◯ DEEP   ◯ NIGHT

DIVE DATA :

TIME IN : ....   TIME OUT : ....

MAX DEPTH : ....

BAR/PS : ....   BAR/PS : ....

TIME OUT : ....   TOTAL TIME : ....

VERIFICATION	NOTES
VERIFICATION SIGNATURE :	....
	....
	....
	....
	....
	....
	....
	....
☐ INSTRUCTOR ☐ DIVEMASTER ☐ BUDDY	

DATE :	
DIVE # :	
COUNTRY :	
LOCATION :	
VISIBILITY :	
WEIGHT :	
CURRENT :	

CONDITIONS :

☀ ☁ 🌧 ⛅
☐ ☐ ☐ ☐

HOT MIDL CLOUD
☐   ☐   ☐

😃 🙂 ☹
☐ ☐ ☐

◯ SALT ◯ FRESH ◯ SHORE ◯ BOAT ◯ DEEP ◯ NIGHT

DIVE DATA :

TIME IN : .... TIME OUT : ....

MAX DEPTH : ....

BAR/PS : .... BAR/PS : ....

TIME OUT : .... TOTAL TIME : ....

VERIFICATION

VERIFICATION SIGNATURE :

◯ INSTRUCTOR ◯ DIVEMASTER ◯ BUDDY

NOTES

....
....
....
....
....
....
....
....

DATE :	
DIVE # :	
COUNTRY :	
LOCATION :	
VISIBILITY :	
WEIGHT :	
CURRENT :	

CONDITIONS :

☀ ☁ 🌧 ⛅
☐ ☐ ☐ ☐

HOT   MIDL   CLOUD
☐   ☐   ☐

😀   🙂   ☹
☐   ☐   ☐

○ SALT ○ FRESH ○ SHORE ○ BOAT ○ DEEP ○ NIGHT

DIVE DATA :

TIME IN : ....   TIME OUT : ....

MAX DEPTH : ....

BAR/PS : ....   BAR/PS : ....

TIME OUT : ....   TOTAL TIME : ....

VERIFICATION

VERIFICATION SIGNATURE :

NOTES

○ INSTRUCTOR   ○ DIVEMASTER   ○ BUDDY

DATE :	
DIVE # :	
COUNTRY :	
LOCATION :	
VISIBILITY :	
WEIGHT :	
CURRENT :	

CONDITIONS :

☀ ☐   ☁ ☐   🌧 ☐   ⛅ ☐

HOT ☐   MIDL ☐   CLOUD ☐

😀 ☐   🙂 ☐   ☹ ☐

◯ SALT ◯ FRESH ◯ SHORE ◯ BOAT ◯ DEEP ◯ NIGHT

DIVE DATA :

TIME IN : ....   TIME OUT : ....

MAX DEPTH : ....

BAR/PS : ....   BAR/PS : ....

TIME OUT : ....   TOTAL TIME : ....

VERIFICATION

VERIFICATION SIGNATURE :

☐ INSTRUCTOR   ☐ DIVEMASTER   ☐ BUDDY

NOTES

....
....
....
....
....
....
....
....

DATE :	
DIVE # :	
COUNTRY :	
LOCATION :	
VISIBILITY :	
WEIGHT :	
CURRENT :	

CONDITIONS :

☀ ☁ 🌧 ⛅
☐ ☐ ☐ ☐

HOT   MIDL   CLOUD
☐   ☐   ☐

😃   🙂   ☹
☐   ☐   ☐

○ SALT ○ FRESH ○ SHORE ○ BOAT ○ DEEP ○ NIGHT

DIVE DATA :

TIME IN : .... TIME OUT : ....

MAX DEPTH : ....

BAR/PS : .... BAR/PS : ....

TIME OUT : .... TOTAL TIME : ....

VERIFICATION

VERIFICATION SIGNATURE :

☐ INSTRUCTOR   ☐ DIVEMASTER   ☐ BUDDY

NOTES

....
....
....
....
....
....
....
....

DATE :	
DIVE # :	
COUNTRY :	
LOCATION :	
VISIBILITY :	
WEIGHT :	
CURRENT :	

CONDITIONS :

☀ ☁ 🌧 ⛅
☐ ☐ ☐ ☐

HOT MIDL CLOUD
☐   ☐   ☐

😀 🙂 ☹
☐ ☐ ☐

○ SALT ○ FRESH ○ SHORE ○ BOAT ○ DEEP ○ NIGHT

DIVE DATA :

TIME IN : ....   TIME OUT : ....

MAX DEPTH : ....

BAR/PS : ....   BAR/PS : ....

TIME OUT : ....   TOTAL TIME : ....

VERIFICATION

VERIFICATION SIGNATURE :

NOTES

....
....
....
....
....
....
....
....

☐ INSTRUCTOR   ☐ DIVEMASTER   ☐ BUDDY

DATE :	
DIVE # :	
COUNTRY :	
LOCATION :	
VISIBILITY :	
WEIGHT :	
CURRENT :	

CONDITIONS :

☀ ☁ 🌧 ⛅
☐ ☐ ☐ ☐

HOT   MIDL   CLOUD
☐   ☐   ☐

😃   🙂   ☹
☐   ☐   ☐

◯ SALT   ◯ FRESH   ◯ SHORE   ◯ BOAT   ◯ DEEP   ◯ NIGHT

DIVE DATA :

TIME IN : ....

TIME OUT : ....

MAX DEPTH : ....

BAR/PS : ....

BAR/PS : ....

TIME OUT : ....

TOTAL TIME : ....

VERIFICATION

VERIFICATION SIGNATURE :

☐ INSTRUCTOR   ☐ DIVEMASTER   ☐ BUDDY

NOTES

DATE :
DIVE # :
COUNTRY :
LOCATION :
VISIBILITY :
WEIGHT :
CURRENT :

CONDITIONS :

☀	☁	🌧	⛅
☐	☐	☐	☐
HOT	MIDL		CLOUD
☐	☐		☐
😃	🙂		☹
☐	☐		☐

○ SALT ○ FRESH ○ SHORE ○ BOAT ○ DEEP ○ NIGHT

DIVE DATA :

TIME IN : .... TIME OUT : ....

MAX DEPTH : ....

BAR/PS : .... BAR/PS : ....

TIME OUT : .... TOTAL TIME : ....

VERIFICATION

VERIFICATION SIGNATURE :

○ INSTRUCTOR ○ DIVEMASTER ○ BUDDY

NOTES

DATE :	**CONDITIONS :**
DIVE # :	☀ ☁ 🌧 ⛅
COUNTRY :	☐ ☐ ☐ ☐
LOCATION :	🌡 🌡 🌡
VISIBILITY :	HOT MIDL CLOUD
WEIGHT :	☐ ☐ ☐
CURRENT :	😀 ☺ ☹
	☐ ☐ ☐

◯ SALT ◯ FRESH ◯ SHORE ◯ BOAT ◯ DEEP ◯ NIGHT

DIVE DATA :

TIME IN : ....   TIME OUT : ....

MAX DEPTH : ....

BAR/PS : ....   BAR/PS : ....

TIME OUT : ....   TOTAL TIME : ....

VERIFICATION	NOTES
VERIFICATION SIGNATURE :	....
	....
	....
	....
	....
	....
	....
	....
☐ INSTRUCTOR ☐ DIVEMASTER ☐ BUDDY	

DATE :	
DIVE # :	
COUNTRY :	
LOCATION :	
VISIBILITY :	
WEIGHT :	
CURRENT :	

CONDITIONS :

☀	☁	🌧	⛅
☐	☐	☐	☐
HOT	MIDL		CLOUD
☐	☐		☐
😃	🙂		☹
☐	☐		☐

◯ SALT   ◯ FRESH   ◯ SHORE   ◯ BOAT   ◯ DEEP   ◯ NIGHT

DIVE DATA :

TIME IN : ....

TIME OUT : ....

MAX DEPTH : ....

BAR/PS : ....

BAR/PS : ....

TIME OUT : ....

TOTAL TIME : ....

VERIFICATION

VERIFICATION SIGNATURE :

☐ INSTRUCTOR   ☐ DIVEMASTER   ☐ BUDDY

NOTES

DATE :	**CONDITIONS :**
DIVE # :	☀ ☁ 🌧 ⛅
COUNTRY :	☐ ☐ ☐ ☐
LOCATION :	HOT MIDL CLOUD
VISIBILITY :	☐ ☐ ☐
WEIGHT :	🙂 🙂 🙁
CURRENT :	☐ ☐ ☐

◯ SALT ◯ FRESH ◯ SHORE ◯ BOAT ◯ DEEP ◯ NIGHT

DIVE DATA :

TIME IN : ....   TIME OUT : ....

MAX DEPTH : ....

BAR/PS : ....   BAR/PS : ....

TIME OUT : ....   TOTAL TIME : ....

VERIFICATION	NOTES
VERIFICATION SIGNATURE :	....
☐ INSTRUCTOR ☐ DIVEMASTER ☐ BUDDY	

DATE :	CONDITIONS :
DIVE # :	☀ ☁ 🌧 ⛅
COUNTRY :	☐ ☐ ☐ ☐
LOCATION :	HOT MIDL CLOUD
VISIBILITY :	☐ ☐ ☐
WEIGHT :	😀 🙂 ☹
CURRENT :	☐ ☐ ☐

○ SALT   ○ FRESH   ○ SHORE   ○ BOAT   ○ DEEP   ○ NIGHT

DIVE DATA :

TIME IN : ....   TIME OUT : ....

MAX DEPTH : ....

BAR/PS : ....   BAR/PS : ....

TIME OUT : ....   TOTAL TIME : ....

VERIFICATION

VERIFICATION SIGNATURE :

☐ INSTRUCTOR   ☐ DIVEMASTER   ☐ BUDDY

NOTES

DATE :

DIVE # :

COUNTRY :

LOCATION :

VISIBILITY :

WEIGHT :

CURRENT :

CONDITIONS :

☀ ☁ 🌧 ⛅
☐ ☐ ☐ ☐

HOT   MIDL   CLOUD
☐   ☐   ☐

😀   🙂   🙁
☐   ☐   ☐

○ SALT   ○ FRESH   ○ SHORE   ○ BOAT   ○ DEEP   ○ NIGHT

DIVE DATA :

TIME IN : ....   TIME OUT : ....

MAX DEPTH : ....

BAR/PS : ....   BAR/PS : ....

TIME OUT : ....   TOTAL TIME : ....

VERIFICATION	NOTES
VERIFICATION SIGNATURE :	

☐ INSTRUCTOR   ☐ DIVEMASTER   ☐ BUDDY

DATE :	
DIVE # :	
COUNTRY :	
LOCATION :	
VISIBILITY :	
WEIGHT :	
CURRENT :	

CONDITIONS :

☀ ☐	☁ ☐	🌧 ☐	⛅ ☐
HOT ☐	MIDL ☐		CLOUD ☐
😃 ☐	🙂 ☐		☹ ☐

○ SALT ○ FRESH ○ SHORE ○ BOAT ○ DEEP ○ NIGHT

DIVE DATA :

TIME IN : .... TIME OUT : ....

MAX DEPTH : ....

BAR/PS : .... BAR/PS : ....

TIME OUT : .... TOTAL TIME : ....

VERIFICATION

VERIFICATION SIGNATURE :

☐ INSTRUCTOR ☐ DIVEMASTER ☐ BUDDY

NOTES

....
....
....
....
....
....
....
....

DATE :	
DIVE # :	
COUNTRY :	
LOCATION :	
VISIBILITY :	
WEIGHT :	
CURRENT :	

CONDITIONS :

☀ ☁ 🌧 ⛅
☐ ☐ ☐ ☐

HOT MIDL CLOUD
☐ ☐ ☐

😀 🙂 ☹
☐ ☐ ☐

○ SALT ○ FRESH ○ SHORE ○ BOAT ○ DEEP ○ NIGHT

DIVE DATA :

TIME IN : ....   TIME OUT : ....

MAX DEPTH : ....

BAR/PS : ....   BAR/PS : ....

TIME OUT : ....   TOTAL TIME : ....

VERIFICATION

VERIFICATION SIGNATURE :

☐ INSTRUCTOR   ☐ DIVEMASTER   ☐ BUDDY

NOTES

....
....
....
....
....
....
....
....

DATE :	
DIVE # :	
COUNTRY :	
LOCATION :	
VISIBILITY :	
WEIGHT :	
CURRENT :	

CONDITIONS :

☀ ☁ 🌧 ⛅
☐ ☐ ☐ ☐

HOT ☐   MIDL ☐   CLOUD ☐

😃 ☐   🙂 ☐   ☹ ☐

○ SALT   ○ FRESH   ○ SHORE   ○ BOAT   ○ DEEP   ○ NIGHT

DIVE DATA :

TIME IN : .... TIME OUT : ....

MAX DEPTH : ....

BAR/PS : .... BAR/PS : ....

TIME OUT : .... TOTAL TIME : ....

VERIFICATION

VERIFICATION SIGNATURE :

☐ INSTRUCTOR   ☐ DIVEMASTER   ☐ BUDDY

NOTES

DATE :	
DIVE # :	
COUNTRY :	
LOCATION :	
VISIBILITY :	
WEIGHT :	
CURRENT :	

CONDITIONS :

☀ ☁ 🌧 ⛅
☐ ☐ ☐ ☐

HOT — MIDL — CLOUD
☐ ☐ ☐

😃 🙂 ☹
☐ ☐ ☐

○ SALT ○ FRESH ○ SHORE ○ BOAT ○ DEEP ○ NIGHT

DIVE DATA :

TIME IN : .... TIME OUT : ....

MAX DEPTH : ....

BAR/PS : .... BAR/PS : ....

TIME OUT : .... TOTAL TIME : ....

VERIFICATION

VERIFICATION SIGNATURE :

NOTES

☐ INSTRUCTOR ☐ DIVEMASTER ☐ BUDDY

DATE :	
DIVE # :	
COUNTRY :	
LOCATION :	
VISIBILITY :	
WEIGHT :	
CURRENT :	

CONDITIONS :

☀ ☁ 🌧 ⛅
☐ ☐ ☐ ☐

HOT MIDL CLOUD
☐   ☐   ☐

😃 🙂 ☹
☐ ☐ ☐

○ SALT   ○ FRESH   ○ SHORE   ○ BOAT   ○ DEEP   ○ NIGHT

DIVE DATA :

TIME IN : .... TIME OUT : ....

MAX DEPTH : ....

BAR/PS : .... BAR/PS : ....

TIME OUT : .... TOTAL TIME : ....

VERIFICATION

VERIFICATION SIGNATURE :

☐ INSTRUCTOR   ☐ DIVEMASTER   ☐ BUDDY

NOTES

....
....
....
....
....
....
....
....
....

DATE :	
DIVE # :	
COUNTRY :	
LOCATION :	
VISIBILITY :	
WEIGHT :	
CURRENT :	

CONDITIONS :

☀ ☁ 🌧 ⛅
☐ ☐ ☐ ☐

HOT   MIDL   CLOUD
☐   ☐   ☐

😀   🙂   ☹
☐   ☐   ☐

○ SALT ○ FRESH ○ SHORE ○ BOAT ○ DEEP ○ NIGHT

DIVE DATA :

TIME IN : ....   TIME OUT : ....

MAX DEPTH : ....

BAR/PS : ....   BAR/PS : ....

TIME OUT : ....   TOTAL TIME : ....

VERIFICATION

VERIFICATION SIGNATURE :

☐ INSTRUCTOR   ☐ DIVEMASTER   ☐ BUDDY

NOTES

....
....
....
....
....
....
....
....

DATE :	
DIVE # :	
COUNTRY :	
LOCATION :	
VISIBILITY :	
WEIGHT :	
CURRENT :	

CONDITIONS :

- ☀ ☐
- ☁ ☐
- 🌧 ☐
- ⛅ ☐

- HOT ☐
- MIDL ☐
- CLOUD ☐

- 😃 ☐
- 🙂 ☐
- ☹ ☐

☐ SALT ☐ FRESH ☐ SHORE ☐ BOAT ☐ DEEP ☐ NIGHT

DIVE DATA :

TIME IN : ....

TIME OUT : ....

MAX DEPTH : ....

BAR/PS : ....

BAR/PS : ....

TIME OUT : ....

TOTAL TIME : ....

VERIFICATION

VERIFICATION SIGNATURE :

NOTES

....
....
....
....
....
....
....
....

☐ INSTRUCTOR ☐ DIVEMASTER ☐ BUDDY

DATE :	
DIVE # :	
COUNTRY :	
LOCATION :	
VISIBILITY :	
WEIGHT :	
CURRENT :	

CONDITIONS :

☀ ☐   ☁ ☐   🌧 ☐   ⛅ ☐

HOT ☐   MIDL ☐   CLOUD ☐

😀 ☐   🙂 ☐   🙁 ☐

○ SALT   ○ FRESH   ○ SHORE   ○ BOAT   ○ DEEP   ○ NIGHT

DIVE DATA :

TIME IN : ....   TIME OUT : ....

MAX DEPTH : ....

BAR/PS : ....   BAR/PS : ....

TIME OUT : ....   TOTAL TIME : ....

VERIFICATION

VERIFICATION SIGNATURE :

☐ INSTRUCTOR   ☐ DIVEMASTER   ☐ BUDDY

NOTES

DATE :	
DIVE # :	
COUNTRY :	
LOCATION :	
VISIBILITY :	
WEIGHT :	
CURRENT :	

CONDITIONS :

☀ ☁ 🌧 ⛅
☐ ☐ ☐ ☐

HOT MIDL CLOUD
☐   ☐   ☐

😀 🙂 ☹
☐ ☐ ☐

☐ SALT ☐ FRESH ☐ SHORE ☐ BOAT ☐ DEEP ☐ NIGHT

DIVE DATA :

TIME IN : .... TIME OUT : ....

MAX DEPTH : ....

BAR/PS : .... BAR/PS : ....

TIME OUT : .... TOTAL TIME : ....

VERIFICATION

VERIFICATION SIGNATURE :

☐ INSTRUCTOR   ☐ DIVEMASTER   ☐ BUDDY

NOTES

....
....
....
....
....
....
....
....

DATE :	CONDITIONS :
DIVE # :	☀ ☁ 🌧 ⛅
COUNTRY :	□ □ □ □
LOCATION :	HOT MIDL CLOUD
VISIBILITY :	□ □ □
WEIGHT :	😃 🙂 ☹
CURRENT :	□ □ □

◯ SALT ◯ FRESH ◯ SHORE ◯ BOAT ◯ DEEP ◯ NIGHT

DIVE DATA :

TIME IN : .... TIME OUT : ....

MAX DEPTH : ....

BAR/PS : .... BAR/PS : ....

TIME OUT : .... TOTAL TIME : ....

VERIFICATION	NOTES
VERIFICATION SIGNATURE :	....
	....
	....
	....
	....
	....
	....
◯ INSTRUCTOR ◯ DIVEMASTER ◯ BUDDY	

DATE :	
DIVE # :	
COUNTRY :	
LOCATION :	
VISIBILITY :	
WEIGHT :	
CURRENT :	

CONDITIONS :

☀ ☁ 🌧 ⛅
☐ ☐ ☐ ☐

HOT   MIDL   CLOUD
☐   ☐   ☐

😀 🙂 ☹
☐ ☐ ☐

○ SALT   ○ FRESH   ○ SHORE   ○ BOAT   ○ DEEP   ○ NIGHT

DIVE DATA :

TIME IN : ....   TIME OUT : ....

MAX DEPTH : ....

BAR/PS : ....   BAR/PS : ....

TIME OUT : ....   TOTAL TIME : ....

VERIFICATION

VERIFICATION SIGNATURE :

☐ INSTRUCTOR   ☐ DIVEMASTER   ☐ BUDDY

NOTES

....
....
....
....
....
....
....
....

DATE :	**CONDITIONS :**
DIVE # :	☀️ ☁️ 🌧️ ⛅
COUNTRY :	□ □ □ □
LOCATION :	🌡️ 🌡️ 🌡️
VISIBILITY :	HOT MIDL CLOUD
WEIGHT :	□ □ □
CURRENT :	😀 🙂 ☹️
	□ □ □

○ SALT ○ FRESH ○ SHORE ○ BOAT ○ DEEP ○ NIGHT

DIVE DATA :

TIME IN : ....   TIME OUT : ....

MAX DEPTH : ....

BAR/PS : ....   BAR/PS : ....

TIME OUT : ....   TOTAL TIME : ....

VERIFICATION	NOTES
VERIFICATION SIGNATURE :	....
	....
	....
	....
	....
	....
	....
	....
□ INSTRUCTOR □ DIVEMASTER □ BUDDY	

DATE :	
DIVE # :	
COUNTRY :	
LOCATION :	
VISIBILITY :	
WEIGHT :	
CURRENT :	

CONDITIONS :

☀ ☁ 🌧 ⛅
☐ ☐ ☐ ☐

HOT MIDL CLOUD
☐ ☐ ☐

😃 🙂 ☹
☐ ☐ ☐

☐ SALT ☐ FRESH ☐ SHORE ☐ BOAT ☐ DEEP ☐ NIGHT

DIVE DATA :

TIME IN : .... TIME OUT : ....

MAX DEPTH : ....

BAR/PS : .... BAR/PS : ....

TIME OUT : .... TOTAL TIME : ....

VERIFICATION

VERIFICATION SIGNATURE :

☐ INSTRUCTOR ☐ DIVEMASTER ☐ BUDDY

NOTES

DATE :	
DIVE # :	
COUNTRY :	
LOCATION :	
VISIBILITY :	
WEIGHT :	
CURRENT :	

CONDITIONS :

☀ ☁ 🌧 ⛅
☐ ☐ ☐ ☐

HOT MIDL CLOUD
☐   ☐   ☐

😀 🙂 ☹
☐ ☐ ☐

○ SALT ○ FRESH ○ SHORE ○ BOAT ○ DEEP ○ NIGHT

DIVE DATA :

TIME IN : .... TIME OUT : ....

MAX DEPTH : ....

BAR/PS : .... BAR/PS : ....

TIME OUT : .... TOTAL TIME : ....

VERIFICATION

VERIFICATION SIGNATURE :

☐ INSTRUCTOR   ☐ DIVEMASTER   ☐ BUDDY

NOTES

....
....
....
....
....
....
....
....

DATE :	
DIVE # :	
COUNTRY :	
LOCATION :	
VISIBILITY :	
WEIGHT :	
CURRENT :	

CONDITIONS :

☀ ☁ 🌧 ⛅
☐ ☐ ☐ ☐

HOT   MIDL   CLOUD
☐   ☐   ☐

😀 🙂 ☹
☐ ☐ ☐

◯ SALT ◯ FRESH ◯ SHORE ◯ BOAT ◯ DEEP ◯ NIGHT

DIVE DATA :

TIME IN : .... TIME OUT : ....

MAX DEPTH : ....

BAR/PS : .... BAR/PS : ....

TIME OUT : .... TOTAL TIME : ....

VERIFICATION

VERIFICATION SIGNATURE :

☐ INSTRUCTOR   ☐ DIVEMASTER   ☐ BUDDY

NOTES

....
....
....
....
....
....
....
....

DATE :	
DIVE # :	
COUNTRY :	
LOCATION :	
VISIBILITY :	
WEIGHT :	
CURRENT :	

CONDITIONS :

☀ ☐   ☁ ☐   🌧 ☐   ⛅ ☐

HOT ☐   MIDL ☐   CLOUD ☐

😃 ☐   🙂 ☐   ☹ ☐

○ SALT   ○ FRESH   ○ SHORE   ○ BOAT   ○ DEEP   ○ NIGHT

DIVE DATA :

TIME IN : .... TIME OUT : ....

MAX DEPTH : ....

BAR/PS : .... BAR/PS : ....

TIME OUT : .... TOTAL TIME : ....

VERIFICATION

VERIFICATION SIGNATURE :

○ INSTRUCTOR   ○ DIVEMASTER   ○ BUDDY

NOTES

....
....
....
....
....
....
....
....

DATE :	
DIVE # :	
COUNTRY :	
LOCATION :	
VISIBILITY :	
WEIGHT :	
CURRENT :	

CONDITIONS :

☀ ☁ 🌧 ⛅
☐ ☐ ☐ ☐

HOT   MIDL   CLOUD
☐   ☐   ☐

😀   🙂   ☹
☐   ☐   ☐

○ SALT ○ FRESH ○ SHORE ○ BOAT ○ DEEP ○ NIGHT

DIVE DATA :

TIME IN : .... TIME OUT : ....

MAX DEPTH : ....

BAR/PS : .... BAR/PS : ....

TIME OUT : .... TOTAL TIME : ....

VERIFICATION

VERIFICATION SIGNATURE :

☐ INSTRUCTOR ☐ DIVEMASTER ☐ BUDDY

NOTES

....
....
....
....
....
....
....
....

DATE :	
DIVE # :	
COUNTRY :	
LOCATION :	
VISIBILITY :	
WEIGHT :	
CURRENT :	

CONDITIONS :

☀ ☁ 🌧 ⛅
☐ ☐ ☐ ☐

HOT MIDL CLOUD
☐   ☐   ☐

😀 🙂 ☹
☐ ☐ ☐

○ SALT ○ FRESH ○ SHORE ○ BOAT ○ DEEP ○ NIGHT

DIVE DATA :

TIME IN : .... TIME OUT : ....

MAX DEPTH : ....

BAR/PS : .... BAR/PS : ....

TIME OUT : .... TOTAL TIME : ....

VERIFICATION

VERIFICATION SIGNATURE :

NOTES

....
....
....
....
....
....
....
....

☐ INSTRUCTOR ☐ DIVEMASTER ☐ BUDDY

DATE :	
DIVE # :	
COUNTRY :	
LOCATION :	
VISIBILITY :	
WEIGHT :	
CURRENT :	

CONDITIONS :

☀ ☐   ☁ ☐   🌧 ☐   ⛅ ☐

HOT ☐   MIDL ☐   CLOUD ☐

😃 ☐   🙂 ☐   ☹ ☐

○ SALT   ○ FRESH   ○ SHORE   ○ BOAT   ○ DEEP   ○ NIGHT

DIVE DATA :

TIME IN : ....   TIME OUT : ....

MAX DEPTH : ....

BAR/PS : ....   BAR/PS : ....

TIME OUT : ....   TOTAL TIME : ....

VERIFICATION

VERIFICATION SIGNATURE :

☐ INSTRUCTOR   ☐ DIVEMASTER   ☐ BUDDY

NOTES

....
....
....
....
....
....
....
....

DATE :	
DIVE # :	
COUNTRY :	
LOCATION :	
VISIBILITY :	
WEIGHT :	
CURRENT :	

CONDITIONS :

☀ ☁ 🌧 ⛅
☐ ☐ ☐ ☐

HOT MIDL CLOUD
☐   ☐   ☐

😀 🙂 ☹
☐ ☐ ☐

○ SALT   ○ FRESH   ○ SHORE   ○ BOAT   ○ DEEP   ○ NIGHT

DIVE DATA :

TIME IN : ....   TIME OUT : ....

MAX DEPTH : ....

BAR/PS : ....   BAR/PS : ....

TIME OUT : ....   TOTAL TIME : ....

VERIFICATION

VERIFICATION SIGNATURE :

☐ INSTRUCTOR   ☐ DIVEMASTER   ☐ BUDDY

NOTES

DATE :	
DIVE # :	
COUNTRY :	
LOCATION :	
VISIBILITY :	
WEIGHT :	
CURRENT :	

CONDITIONS :

☀ ☐ ☁ ☐ 🌧 ☐ ⛅ ☐

HOT ☐   MIDL ☐   CLOUD ☐

😃 ☐   🙂 ☐   ☹ ☐

◯ SALT   ◯ FRESH   ◯ SHORE   ◯ BOAT   ◯ DEEP   ◯ NIGHT

DIVE DATA :

TIME IN : ....   TIME OUT : ....

MAX DEPTH : ....

BAR/PS : ....   BAR/PS : ....

TIME OUT : ....   TOTAL TIME : ....

VERIFICATION

VERIFICATION SIGNATURE :

☐ INSTRUCTOR   ☐ DIVEMASTER   ☐ BUDDY

NOTES

....
....
....
....
....
....
....
....

DATE :	
DIVE # :	
COUNTRY :	
LOCATION :	
VISIBILITY :	
WEIGHT :	
CURRENT :	

CONDITIONS :

☀ ☐	☁☁ ☐	🌧 ☐	⛅ ☐
HOT ☐	MIDL ☐		CLOUD ☐
😃 ☐	🙂 ☐		☹ ☐

○ SALT   ○ FRESH   ○ SHORE   ○ BOAT   ○ DEEP   ○ NIGHT

DIVE DATA :

TIME IN : ....   TIME OUT : ....

MAX DEPTH : ....

BAR/PS : ....   BAR/PS : ....

TIME OUT : ....   TOTAL TIME : ....

VERIFICATION

VERIFICATION SIGNATURE :

☐ INSTRUCTOR   ☐ DIVEMASTER   ☐ BUDDY

NOTES

....
....
....
....
....
....
....
....

DATE :	
DIVE # :	
COUNTRY :	
LOCATION :	
VISIBILITY :	
WEIGHT :	
CURRENT :	

CONDITIONS :

☀ ☁ 🌧 ⛅
☐ ☐ ☐ ☐

HOT   MIDL   CLOUD
☐   ☐   ☐

😀   🙂   ☹
☐   ☐   ☐

○ SALT ○ FRESH ○ SHORE ○ BOAT ○ DEEP ○ NIGHT

DIVE DATA :

TIME IN : ....   TIME OUT : ....

MAX DEPTH : ....

BAR/PS : ....   BAR/PS : ....

TIME OUT : ....   TOTAL TIME : ....

VERIFICATION

VERIFICATION SIGNATURE :

☐ INSTRUCTOR   ☐ DIVEMASTER   ☐ BUDDY

NOTES

DATE :	**CONDITIONS :**
DIVE # :	☀️ ☁️ 🌧️ ⛅
COUNTRY :	□ □ □ □
LOCATION :	HOT MIDL CLOUD
VISIBILITY :	□ □ □
WEIGHT :	😃 🙂 ☹️
CURRENT :	□ □ □

◯ SALT ◯ FRESH ◯ SHORE ◯ BOAT ◯ DEEP ◯ NIGHT

DIVE DATA :

TIME IN : ....   TIME OUT : ....

MAX DEPTH : ....

BAR/PS : ....   BAR/PS : ....

TIME OUT : ....   TOTAL TIME : ....

VERIFICATION	NOTES
VERIFICATION SIGNATURE :	....
	....
	....
	....
	....
	....
	....
	....
☐ INSTRUCTOR ☐ DIVEMASTER ☐ BUDDY	

DATE :	
DIVE # :	
COUNTRY :	
LOCATION :	
VISIBILITY :	
WEIGHT :	
CURRENT :	

CONDITIONS :

☀ ☐   ☁ ☐   🌧 ☐   ⛅ ☐

HOT ☐   MIDL ☐   CLOUD ☐

😃 ☐   🙂 ☐   ☹ ☐

○ SALT ○ FRESH ○ SHORE ○ BOAT ○ DEEP ○ NIGHT

DIVE DATA :

TIME IN : ....   TIME OUT : ....

MAX DEPTH : ....

BAR/PS : ....   BAR/PS : ....

TIME OUT : ....   TOTAL TIME : ....

VERIFICATION

VERIFICATION SIGNATURE :

○ INSTRUCTOR   ○ DIVEMASTER   ○ BUDDY

NOTES

....
....
....
....
....
....
....
....

DATE :	
DIVE # :	
COUNTRY :	
LOCATION :	
VISIBILITY :	
WEIGHT :	
CURRENT :	

CONDITIONS :

☀ ☁ 🌧 ⛅
☐ ☐ ☐ ☐

HOT ☐   MIDL ☐   CLOUD ☐

😀 ☐   🙂 ☐   ☹ ☐

○ SALT ○ FRESH ○ SHORE ○ BOAT ○ DEEP ○ NIGHT

DIVE DATA :

TIME IN : .... TIME OUT : ....

MAX DEPTH : ....

BAR/PS : .... BAR/PS : ....

TIME OUT : .... TOTAL TIME : ....

VERIFICATION

VERIFICATION SIGNATURE :

☐ INSTRUCTOR   ☐ DIVEMASTER   ☐ BUDDY

NOTES

....
....
....
....
....
....
....
....
....

DATE :	
DIVE # :	
COUNTRY :	
LOCATION :	
VISIBILITY :	
WEIGHT :	
CURRENT :	

CONDITIONS :

☀ ☐   ☁ ☐   🌧 ☐   ⛅ ☐

HOT ☐   MIDL ☐   CLOUD ☐

😃 ☐   🙂 ☐   ☹ ☐

○ SALT   ○ FRESH   ○ SHORE   ○ BOAT   ○ DEEP   ○ NIGHT

DIVE DATA :

TIME IN : ....

TIME OUT : ....

MAX DEPTH : ....

BAR/PS : ....

BAR/PS : ....

TIME OUT : ....

TOTAL TIME : ....

VERIFICATION

VERIFICATION SIGNATURE :

☐ INSTRUCTOR   ☐ DIVEMASTER   ☐ BUDDY

NOTES

....
....
....
....
....
....
....
....

www.ingramcontent.com/pod-product-compliance
Lightning Source LLC
Chambersburg PA
CBHW070339120526
44590CB00017B/2952